Ston
Fascinating Facts For Kids

Arthur Jackman

This book is just one of a series of "Fascinating Facts For Kids" books. For more fascinating facts about people, history, animals and much more please visit:

www.fascinatingfactsforkids.com

Contents

What is Stonehenge?

1. Stonehenge is one of the most famous prehistoric monuments in the world. It is a circle of large, heavy stones which were put in place thousands of years ago.

2. Nobody knows for sure why Stonehenge was built, but it is likely that the ancient Britons gathered there to carry out religious ceremonies.

3. Stonehenge stands on Salisbury Plain in the south-east of England, around 80 miles (130 km) west of London. Salisbury Plain is a large, open area of land with few trees, which means that the impressive sight of Stonehenge can be seen for miles around.

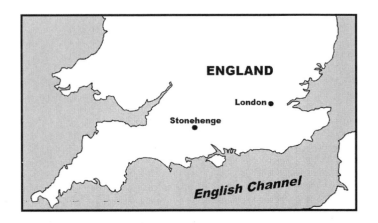

4. Stonehenge isn't the only stone circle in Britain, although it is certainly the most famous. Stone circles seem to have been very important to the ancient Britons as there are hundreds of surviving examples to be found throughout the British Isles.

A stone circle at Castlerigg in northern England

Who Built Stonehenge?

5.   The building of Stonehenge took place over a period of around 1,500 years with three different tribes of people bringing their own ideas and changes to the construction of the monument. These three tribes were the Windmill Hill people, the Beaker people and the Wessex people.

6.   The Windmill Hill people lived on Salisbury Plain around 3,000 BC and were one of the first civilizations to produce their food by farming, rather than hunting animals and gathering fruit and berries. They were an advanced civilization, which is part of the reason it is thought they began the building of Stonehenge.

7.   The Beaker people migrated from mainland Europe to settle in Britain around 2,500 BC. They get their name from the pottery drinking vessels - or 'beakers' - they buried with their dead. Along with Stonehenge, the Beaker people built many more of Britain's stone circles.

8.   The Wessex people arrived on Salisbury Plain around 1,500 BC. They were a very advanced culture and are thought to have been responsible for the final stages of the construction of Stonehenge.

How Was Stonehenge Built?

9. The first Stonehenge was begun more than 5,000 years ago in around 3,000 BC. The first builders dug a huge circular ditch around 300 feet (100 m) in diameter using simple tools made from deer antlers and the shoulder bones of cows.

10. The soil that was dug up was used to build two six-foot high (2 m) banks on either side of the ditch. A gap was left in the banks to provide an entrance into the circle.

11. Inside the circular ditch 56 holes were dug which are known today as the Aubrey Holes. They are named after John Aubrey, the 17th century archaeologist who discovered them.

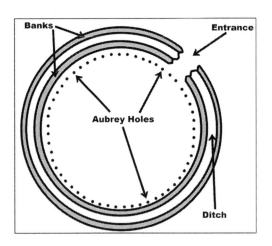

The first Stonehenge with the Aubrey Holes

12. The Aubrey Holes were around three feet (1 m) deep and wide and although nobody knows for sure why they were dug, it is possible that they may have held wooden posts.

13. It is thought that the first version of Stonehenge was used for around 500 years before being abandoned. It wasn't until around 2,300 BC that the Beaker people began the construction of the second Stonehenge.

14. The second Stonehenge saw a dramatic change from the first version when the first stones arrived. 80 massive bluestones were placed inside the site forming two circles, one inside the other.

15. The bluestones came from the Preseli Hills, 140 miles (225 km) away in South Wales. Why these bluestones were used is not known, but it is thought that the ancient Britons believed they had special powers.

16. To transport the bluestones from Wales to Salisbury Plain would have been a massive undertaking. They would have to have been brought by sea and river before being dragged for miles overland to reach Stonehenge.

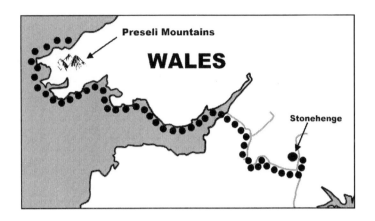

The route from Wales

17. Many experts think that transporting huge, heavy stones on such a long journey would have been impossible. Another theory as to how the stones got to Stonehenge is that they were transported from Wales to somewhere near Salisbury Plain by glaciers during the last ice age.

18. Around the time of the bluestones being put in place, an avenue connecting Stonehenge with the nearby River Avon was constructed. Perhaps this avenue could have been used to transport the bluestones from the river to their final destination?

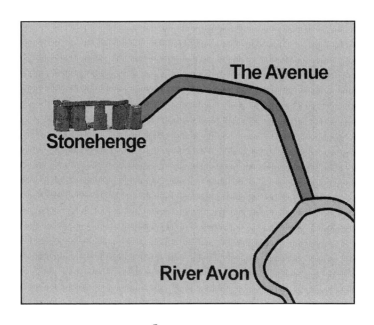

The Avenue

19. The third stage of Stonehenge began around 2,000 BC with the arrival of huge blocks of sarsen - which is a kind of sandstone.

20. The sarsen stones came from quarries around 25 miles (40 km) from Stonehenge, and were probably transported using sledges and ropes. It would have taken hundreds of men to pull just one of the stones from the quarry to Salisbury Plain.

21. The sarsen stones were arranged in a circle and on top of the stones lintels were placed, which spanned the space between each sarsen.

Inside the circle more sarsens were arranged in the shape of a horseshoe.

Sarsen stones with lintels

Building the Stone Circles

22. Once the stones had arrived at Stonehenge, each one had to be made into the right shape before being put into place. Archaeologists have found primitive tools on the site which were used to get each stone the correct size and shape.

23. To get an upright sarsen in place, a deep hole was dug for each stone. Each ditch had a slant on one side which the huge stones were slid down.

24. When the stone was resting on the bottom of its hole, a large wooden frame was placed by it and a large team of men pulled on ropes passing over the frame to pull the stone upright.

25. To get a lintel 20 feet (6 m) into the air to be placed across the top of a sarsen was a difficult and dangerous job. It is possible that a lintel was placed on top of a layer of logs next to the upright stone. It would then be raised at each end to allow a new layer of logs to be put in place. Repeating this process many times would get the lintel to the right height before it could be moved sideways into place on top of the upright stone.

26. Each one of the upright stones had a lump on top. A lintel had two hollows carved into it, one near each end. The bumps in the standing stones fitted into the hollows to hold the lintel in place.

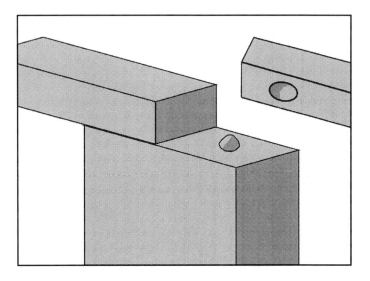

How the lintels and upright stones fitted together

Why Was Stonehenge Built?

27.   Stonehenge was built so long ago - it is even older then the pyramids of ancient Egypt - that nobody can know for sure why it was built and what purpose it served. But it took so much work to build it that it must have been very important to the ancient Britons.

28.   Stonehenge was probably used for different purposes at different times in its history. Many experts think it was once a ceremonial site for the dead. There are many burial sites close to Stonehenge and the dead may have been brought to the monument before being buried.

29.   The ancient Britons believed the bluestones of Stonehenge had healing powers and some experts believe that people came from far and wide to be cured of their illnesses.

30. The Beaker people believed that the Sun held a special power over their lives and they could have used Stonehenge as a temple to worship the Sun. They may have held special ceremonies on Midsummer's Day and Midwinter's Day.

31. The Sun was important to the ancient Britons and it has been discovered that the stones of Stonehenge are placed to line up with the Sun on the shortest and longest days of the year.

32. In the avenue which connects Stonehenge with the River Avon stands a 16-foot-high (5 m) stone called the Heel Stone. On the longest day of the year - the summer solstice - the Sun rises directly over the Heel Stone and its rays shine right into the center of the monument. On the shortest day of the year - the winter solstice - the Sun sets directly opposite the Heel Stone.

The Heel Stone

33. The ancient Britons knew about the movements of the Moon around the Earth and it is thought they used this knowledge when building Stonehenge to predict eclipses of the Sun. A solar eclipse happens when the Moon passes in front of the Sun and blocks sunlight from reaching the Earth.

A solar eclipse

Stonehenge Myths

34. One myth about Stonehenge tells of the monument being built by the legendary wizard, Merlin. It is said that he brought the stones from Ireland and made himself 20 feet (6 m) tall to lift the stones into place. Even if Merlin had such powers he couldn't have built Stonehenge, as according to legend, he lived thousands of years after Stonehenge had been built.

35. People used to think Stonehenge was built by the Romans to be used as a place of worship. But the Romans came to Britain in 40 AD when Stonehenge had been a ruin for centuries.

36. It used to be thought that Stonehenge was built by ancient priests and poets known as the Druids. But the first Druids didn't appear until 2,000 years after Stonehenge was built.

Ancient Druids

37. Some people believe that Stonehenge was built by aliens from another planet as a landing site for their spacecraft, and many sightings of UFOs have been reported there. In 1954 a beam of light seemed to rise from the middle of the monument and in 1977 a mysterious line of lights was filmed in the sky overhead. There have been many other instances of strange events at Stonehenge over the years.

Tourists at Stonehenge

38. People have been visiting Stonehenge for centuries to marvel at the amazing sight of its ruins and it became a popular place for day trips and picnics. Children used to climb the stones and coins were thrown on top of the lintels for good luck.

39. In the late 19th century, modern Druids began to use Stonehenge to celebrate the summer solstice and it became a big annual attraction. But over the years the event became rowdy with people climbing all over the stones and smashing glass bottles. A fence was built round Stonehenge and people were made to pay an admission fee.

Druids celebrating

40. Even though they had to pay to see the stones, thousands of people still visited Stonehenge, turning the ground to mud and damaging the stones. Eventually, people were not allowed to walk among the stones except during the summer and winter solstices.

41. These days, around 1 million people visit Stonehenge every year. They are taken by bus from a visitor center a mile and a half away (2.5 km) where they can look at the stones from a path outside the monument.

Assorted Stonehenge Facts

42. The word 'henge' is a very old word that means 'circular ditch' and Stonehenge isn't the only henge on Salisbury Plain. Two miles (3 km) from Stonehenge is 'Woodhenge', which was discovered when an airplane flew overhead in 1925.

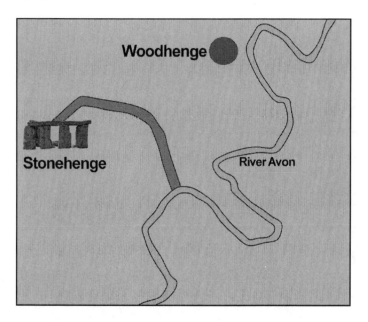

43. Some people believe that Stonehenge was built at the center of a network of 'ley lines', which are thought to be lines of energy that connect many sacred sites throughout the world. This would make Stonehenge an ancient place of power, although not everybody agrees that ley lines exist.

44. British archaeologist professor Richard Atkinson was in charge of excavations at Stonehenge in the 1950s and was a leading authority on the monument. When asked the purpose of Stonehenge, he replied, "There is one short, simple and perfectly correct answer. We do not know and we shall probably never know."

Illustration Attributions

The first Stonehenge with the Aubrey Holes
Adamsan. Copied from en:Image:Stonehenge phase one.jpg

The Heel Stone
Heikki Immonen

Ancient Druids
{{PD-1923}}

Druids celebrating
sandyraidy

Printed in Great Britain
by Amazon